The Otterhound

– A Complete Anthology of the Dog –

1860-1940

ISBN No.
978-14455-2636-2 (Paperback)
978-14455-2756-7 (Hardback)

British Library Cataloguing-in-Publication Data
A catalogue record for this book is available from
the British Library

VDB

www.vintagedogbooks.com

Contents

Containing chapters from the following sources:

The Otter-hound.

The Otter is now often hunted with packs of nondescript hounds. A Bull-terrier, crossed with the rough Scotch or Skye Terrier, makes an excellent dog for this purpose. There are a few packs, however, where the true breed is preserved, and many more where the hounds are in part descended from it.

In real Otter hounds the *forehead* is high, the ears long, full and pendulous, and set far apart on the head.

The *height* is about that of an ordinary Foxhound.

The *coat* is rough and wiry, but comparatively smooth on the upper part of the head; above the jaws it is thick, as in the Deerhound or Scotch Terrier. The colour varies in different packs, but is generally sandy or reddish.

The *jaw* is deep and strong, and the frame powerful. Their note is deep and melodious.

This breed, unlike other hounds, is savage and quarrelsome, and it is sometimes difficult to keep the peace in their kennels.

These fine animals probably more nearly resemble the ancient breeds of English hounds, than any we now possess : they are admirably represented in Landseer's well-known picture, "The Death of the Otter."

THE OTTER HOUND.

This hound, by an oversight, was entirely overlooked in the first edition of the "Dogs of the British Islands," although there are few breeds of a more distinct character and type. Packs of these hounds possess a great advantage in being able to show sport during the summer, and by some it is alleged that otter hunting and angling may be made to dovetail with each other on alternate days of the week; but this is scarcely practicable, inasmuch as the artificial preservation of the otter, in any considerable numbers, is antagonistic to the preservation of the fish on which he wastefully feeds. The angler consequently shows him no mercy, and

MR. CARRICK'S OTTER HOUND "STANLEY."

on " good rivers " the appearance of an otter is the signal for a foray against him with gun, trap, and spear. In Cumberland, Devonshire, and some parts of Wales there are, however, many large brooks and embryo rivers, where the fish run too small for good sport with the rod, and yet afford the otter sufficient food. Here hunting him is prosecuted with great zest, and no one can possibly object to such an amount of preservation as will not supply the adjacent districts with more than a casual visitor, whose appearance is soon signalled to the master of the nearest pack, and a short shrift is given him when once his " spraint " is discovered there. It is alleged by many good sportsmen that the otter does little or no damage to a fishery, but the above is the general impression among the angling fraternity.

The otter hound is no doubt a lineal descendant of the southern hound, with his coat roughened by a long process of selection and careful breeding. He evidently has not been crossed with any breed other than hound, or he would have lost some one or more of the characteristics peculiar to the hunting dog, either in shape of body, length of ear, style of hunting, or tongue. In all these qualities he is a southern hound to the letter, with the addition of a rough coat, the history of which is not known. In many cases a pure foxhound has been used with success against the otter, and, as far as the mere hunting goes, he fulfils the task set him admirably ; but it has usually been found that in a very short time the wet tells on him, and he either becomes rheumatic or is attacked by disease of the chest in some shape. It is not the long hair of the true otter hound which saves him from these penalties, but the thick woolly under-coat, with which he is furnished for the same purpose as in the colley and Dandy Dinmont terrier. He also strongly resembles the southern hound in his style of hunting, which is low and slow, but very sure, his nose being of the tenderest kind, and often owning an air bubble or " vent " at the distance of some yards. Like him, he is apt to sit down on his haunches and throw his tongue with delight at first touching on a scent, as is shown in the engraving in a most characteristic manner. Subscription packs of otter hounds are kept at Carlisle under the mastership of Mr. Carrick; in North-umberland, near Morpeth, under Mr. A. Fenwick; and at Cockermouth, hunted by a committee. In South Wales, Col. Pryse and Mr. Moore have each a pack; while in England the Hon. Geoffrey Hill hunts the otter from his kennels at Hawkeston, Salop, and Mr. Collier's from Culmstock, near Wellington. In the west, Mr. Cheriton and Mr. Mildmay also pursue the sport.

The points of the otter hound are like those of the bloodhound, except as to the coat, which should be composed of hard and long hair, somewhat rough in its lying, and mixed with a short, woolly under-coat, which serves to keep the body warm even when wetted by long immersion. The colour differs also in not being confined to black-and-tan or tan—the former, however, being often met with, as in the case of Mr. Carrick's Stanley, whose portrait accompanies this article. This dog is of a grizzled black-and-tan colour, and of a very fine shape both in head and body. He is by Mr. Carrick's Ringwood out of Harrison's Glory, and took several first prizes at Glasgow, Birmingham, and Nottingham in 1872-3.

5

THE OTTER-HOUND.

ALL writers on the dog, both ancient and modern, who in any way direct attention to the Otter-hound, are unanimous in fathering him on to the old Southern Hound. For our own part we can find no reasons for disagreeing with the opinions of those who have gone before us, though the difference in appearance between the modern Otter-hound and the ancient Southern Hound is very conspicuous as regards coat and colour. In his marking, all old pictures which we have come across portray the old Southern Hound as a coarse Stag or Fox hound, and certainly his similarity to these breeds is greater than it is to the Otter-hound, though the latter is, we believe, one of his descendants.

We have it on the authority of Youatt that it was the slowness of the Southern Hound which led to his falling into disrepute amongst huntsmen, who preferred short sharp bursts to a plodding day across country. Devonshire is popularly believed to have the honour of being the last county in England where a pack of these hounds was kept up; and after its dispersion a number of its members remained for years in the neighbourhood of a village called Aveton Gifford, which is situated in that county. As Devonshire now produces many good specimens of the Otter-hound, this may be regarded as lending additional strength to the theory that the Otter-hound is descended from the former breed.

The precise date of the introduction of the Southern Hound into this country it is impossible to ascertain, and even an approximate guess will be found a matter of difficulty, as no mention is made of this variety in the earliest references to the dogs of Britain. Shakespeare would appear to be alluding to this breed when he writes :—

> " My hounds are bred out of the Spartan kind
> So flewed, so sanded ; and their heads are hung
> With ears that sweep away the morning dew,
> Crook-kneed and dew-lapped like Thessalian bulls,
> Slow in pursuit, but matched in mouth like bells,
> Each unto each."

The allusion to the slowness of the hound alluded to by our national poet is to our minds a convincing proof that it was the Southern Hound which he had in view ; and his reference to its Spartan origin would lead one to presume that its importation into this country was in his day an accepted fact.

Mr. W. Taplin, writing in the "Sportsman's Cabinet," in 1804, has, however, many good words to say for the Southern Hound, and stoutly maintains that although it was less frequently met with in the country than it had been, it was still in existence. To quote his own words, Mr. Taplin remarks—

" These hounds were once universally known and equally common in every part of the kingdom, and the breed were then much larger than those now to be found in the low and marshy parts of the country, where they are still in use for the purposes of the chase, although it has been said 'that the breed, which has been gradually declining, and its size studiously diminished, by a mixture of other kinds, in order to increase its speed, is now almost extinct.' The assertion of the author, however, savours much more of speculative conjecture than of experimental practice; for the present writer hunted the winter of 1775 in the neighbourhood of Manchester with each of the two packs supported by subscription in that town, one of which was denominated the Southern Hound."

Further on the same writer proceeds to remark that "the Southern (or old English Hound) is most undoubtedly the original real-bred Harrier of this country, and more particularly in those swampy parts where the chase is wished to be protracted without prolonging the distance."

In appearance the Southern Hound was a large majestic-looking dog, showing great power, with a long barrel, round ribs, and deep chest. His ears were long, and his voice very melodious, the prevailing colour being, as we have mentioned before, similar to that of the modern Foxhound.

That otter-hunting was conducted on very much the same principles in days gone by as it is in the year 1880, the following extract from Turberville's "Arte de Venerie" will clearly prove; and it is therefore only reasonable to surmise that although the hounds now in use are altered in many respects from the breed used then, the Southern Hound had begun to undergo that modification which has subsequently developed into the modern Otter-hound.

Turberville writes, in 1575 :—

"The otter is a beast well knowne; shee feedeth on fishe and lyeth neare unto ryvers, brookes, pooles, and fishe-ponds, or weares. Hir lying-in commonly is under the roots of trees, and sometimes I have seene them lying in a hollowe tree, foure or five foote above the grounde. Even as a foxe, polcat, wildecat, or badgerd will destroye a warren, so will the otter destroye all the fishe in your pondes, if she once have founde the waye to them. She dyveth and hunteth under the water after a wonderfull manner, so that no fishe can escape hir unlesse they be verie great and swift. A litter of otters will destroy you all the fishe in a ryver in two myles length. There is great cunning in the hunting of them, as shall be saide in the next chapter; and also it is possible to take them under the water, and by the ryver's side, both in traps and in snares, as you may take a hare with hare-pypes, or such like gynnes. They byte sore and venomously, and defende themselves stoutly. I will not speake much more of their nature, but onely that they are footed lyke a goose. I meane they have a webbe betweene theyr clawes, and have no heele, but onely a rounde ball under their soale of their foote, and their tracke is called the marke of an otter, as we say the slot of an hart. An otter abideth not much nor long in one place, but if she befrayed, or finde any fault (as they are very perfectly of smelling and hearing) they will forsake their couche and shifte a mile or two up or doune a river. The like will she do if she have once destroyed the store of fishe, and finde no plentie of feeding. From a pond garden or good store of fish pondes she wil not lightly be removed, as long as there is store of fish in them, for therein fishes are taken with more ease than in the rivers or greater waters; but inough of their natures.

"When a huntesman would hunte the otter, he should first send foure servants or varlets

9

with bloodhounds, or such houndes as will draw in the game, and let him sende them two up the river, and two doune the river, the one couple of them on that one side, and the other on that other side of the water. And so you shal be sure to finde if there be an otter in the quarter: for an otter cannot long abide in the water, but muste come forth in the night to feede on grasse and herbes by the water's side. If any of theyr houndes finde of an otter, let the huntesman looke in the softe groundes and moyst places to see which way he bent the head, up or doune the river. And if he finde not the otter quickly, he may then judge that he is gone to couche somewhere further off from the water, for an otter will sometimes seeke his feede a myle (or little lesse) from his couche and place of reste. Commonly he will rather go up the river than doune, for goyng up the streame, the streame bringeth him sent of the fishes that are above him; and bearing his nose into the winde, he shall the sooner finde any faulte that is above him. Also you should make an assembly for the otter as you do for the harte; and it is a note to be observed, that all such chaces as you draw after, before you finde them, lodge them or herbor them, you shoulde make a solemne assembly to heare all reportes before you undertake to hunte them, and then he which hath found of an otter, or so drawen toward his couche that he can undertake to bryng you unto him, shall cause his houndes to be uncoupled, a bowshotte or twyane before he come to the place where he thinketh that the otter lieth. Because they may cast about a while untill they have cooled their bauling and hainsicke toyes, whiche all houndes do lightly use at the first uncoupling. Then the varlets of the kennell shall seeke by the riverside, and beate the bankes with their houndes untill someone of them chaunce upon the otter.

"Remember always to set out some upwards and some doune the streames, and every man his otter-speare or forked staffe in his hande. And if they perceyve where the otter cometh under water (as they may perceyve if they marke it well) then shall they watche to see if they can get to stand before him at some place where he would vent, and stryke him with theyr speare or staffe. And if they misse then shall they runne up or doune the streame as they see the otter bende, until they may at last give him a blowe. For if the houndes be good otter-houndes, and perfectly entered, they will come chaunting and trayling alongst by the riverside, and will beate every tree roote, every holme, every osier-bedde, and tuft of bullrushes; yea, sometimes also they will take the ryver and beate it like a water-spaniell, so that it shall not be possible for the otter to escape; but that eyther the houndes shall light upon him, or els some of the huntesmen shall strike him, and thus you may have excellent sporte and pastime in hunting of the otter, if the houndes be good, and that the rivers be not over great.

"Where the rivers be great, some use to have a lyne throwen overthwart the river, the whiche two of the huntesmen shall holde by eche ende, one on the one side of the river, and the other on that other. And let them holde the line so slacke that it may alwayes be underneath the water. And if the otter come diving under the water, he shall of necessitie touche their line, and so they shall feele and know which way he is passed, the which shall make him be taken the sooner. An otter's skinne is very good furre, and his grease will make a medicine to make fishes turn up their bellies as if they were deade. A good otter-hound may prove an excellent good buck-hound, if he be not old before he be entered."

In modern days the pack of Otter-hounds hunted by Mr. J. C. Carrick of Carlisle is the leading one in the kingdom, and annually provides excellent sport for the members of the hunt. Mr. Carrick, who is a constant exhibitor at the principal shows, is in the habit of entering some of the members of his pack whenever there is a class for them, and with almost invariable success. His well-known dog Lottery, whose portrait we give, as portraying exactly what an Otter-hound should be in our opinion, was bred by his owner in 1876, and is in colour a fawn grizzle. He is by Lucifer out of Countess, and has won at Darlington and Birmingham on more than one occasion. Lottery measures as follows : Length of head, 10½ inches ; girth of muzzle, 11 inches ; girth of skull, 17 inches ; girth round chest, 30 inches ; height at shoulder, 24 inches ; girth of forearm, 7 inches ; length of stern, 17 inches ; weight, 78 lbs.

MR. CARRICK'S OTTER-HOUND, "LOTTERY."

Many writers on dogs have described the modern Otter-hound as in appearance very closely resembling the Bloodhound. We fail to see the likeness except in the conical skull, and consider that the Otter-hound is a far thicker-made dog than the Bloodhound—at all events, we think he *appears* so. No doubt his rough jacket increases the cloddiness of his build, and depreciates from his naturally symmetrical outline, and for that very reason we dislike the comparison between the two hounds. In Otter-hounds

The Head is big, high, and rather broad.

The Eyes dark and intelligent.

The Ears thin, and hanging flat to the head.

The Shoulders sloping and very muscular.

The Body big, powerful, and well ribbed up.

The Legs very straight, heavily boned, and set on well under the dog.

The Feet large, to assist the dog in the water.

11

The Stern of a fair length, and carried gaily.
The Coat very hard, so as to keep off the wet as much as possible.
The Colour usually grizzle, or fawn grizzle.

SCALE OF POINTS FOR JUDGING OTTER-HOUNDS.

Head and eyes	10
Ears	5
Body and shoulders	10
Legs	5
Feet	5
Coat	10
General appearance, including colour	5
	50

THE OTTER HOUND.

THERE is no finer type of the canine race in this country than the otter hound. His hardy, characteristic expression, shaggy coat, and rough wear and tear appearance, have always reminded me of that ancient British warrior so often depicted in our boyish story books, but who, perhaps, with his coat of skins, his shield, and hirsute face, was the invention of the artist rather than the actual inhabitant of our island.

It has been said that the otter hound is a cross between the Welsh harrier, the southern hound, and the terrier. Perhaps he may be so, but more likely not, for a good well-grown specimen has more coat than any ordinary terrier or the rough Welsh hound, and he is bigger than either. My own opinion is that he has been crossed with the bloodhound at some not very remote date. The black and tan colour often appears in some strains, and his voice in many cases resembles the full, luscious tones of

the bloodhound more than the keener ring of the foxhound. Prior to the outbreak of the Franco-German war, Count de Canteleu sent a number of French griffons to Scotland, where it is said that they were dispersed throughout the country. However, I have not been able to trace their blood in any of our modern hounds. Still, these French hounds would no doubt have been very useful for that purpose. Some twenty-five years or so ago, Mr. J. C. Carrick, of Carlisle, was desirous of getting a fresh cross into his pack, and, with that intention, obtained a hound—a southern hound it was called—from the Western States of America. No pedigree could be obtained, but it was a particularly handsome animal, and more like the picture of the southern hound in Youatt's book on the dog than anything I ever saw. Mr. Carrick was afraid of the fresh blood, so the Virginian importation did good duty on the show bench in the variety classes instead of impurifying a pedigree which was quite as free from taint as that of any other variety of the dog.

I forget who recommended a cross between a bulldog, an Irish water spaniel, and a mastiff, as the most likely way to produce otter hounds. Certainly an ingenious idea, and worthy of the writer, who thus easily got out of a difficulty which more practical and learned men than he had failed to solve. We have the otter hound, let that suffice, and let his valued strain be perpetuated, and the popular masters of our packs long continue to give the best of all sport to those somewhat impecunious individuals who are not provided with the means to keep a hunter or two to gallop after foxhounds. Forty or fifty years ago otter hunting appeared to be on the wane. Perhaps the rising generation of sportsmen of that era became discontented with the nets and spears that were commonly used to facilitate the kill. These cruel appliances are now abolished, and the only place fit to contain them is the lumber room or the museum of some country town. Hounds are so bred that they can, with a minimum amount of assistance, kill their otter unaided, and specially excel iñ their work during the early part of the hunt, if they are but let alone.

Throw off on the river's brink, and hounds will soon hit the line of an otter, if one has been about any time within three or four hours before, or maybe they will speak to scent even older than that. The olfactory organs possessed by the otter hound have, to me, always seemed something extraordinary. The cold, damp stones by the water's edge, or a bunch or clump of grass adjoining, are not the places where scent would lie well. Still, there is the fact : a hound will swim off to a rock in mid-stream, put his nose to the ground, sniff about a little, and, if the otter has been at that spot even for only half a minute, that hound will throw up his head and, in a solo so sweet to the ears of a hunter, let all know that he is on the line.

And it was " Ragman " who never told a lie—can I call him a canine George Washington, without disparagement to America's great president ? I have seen foxhounds well entered to the otter, but the rough hounds were always first to own a stale drag. The latter are so much more staid and steady when past their puppyhood ; know their work so well, appear to enjoy it too, and take to hunting their favoured game at quite an early age.

It is stated of the Rev. John Russell, the great Devonshire sportsman, that, desirous of having a pack of hounds to hunt the otter, he endeavoured to make one. He said he followed the rivers for two seasons, during which he walked upwards of three thousand miles, and never found an otter, although he says " he must have passed scores, and he might as well have searched for a moose deer." No doubt the popular clergyman's foxhounds had been entered to fox. Now, with even a lot of otter hound puppies quite unentered, he would not have had such long and fruitless journeys ; they would soon have hunted something, and if now and then they had run riot on a water rat, a moor hen, or a rabbit, they would have struck the scent of an otter before very long— *i.e.*, if such game were plentiful in the district.

My early experience of otter hunting was much sooner consummated than that of the Devonshire sportsman. We had an otter hound puppy, quite unentered, an old bitch, dam to the puppy, and a few terriers. The second time out we struck a strong scent by the edge of a lovely stream in our north country. Old Rally, who, later on, very often failed to speak, even on a strong scent, now gave tongue freely; her young son put his nose to the ground, threw up his head, and yelled every now and then, and quite as often fell head over heels into the water; the terriers yelped and barked, and evidently thought they were in for a big rat battue.

The young hound settled down and swam across the pool. Higher, Rally marked under a tree root. An angler hard by prodded his landing-net handle down into the ground; all of us jumped upon the surface, and quietly there dived out a huge otter! And he made his way down stream. Then we had him in a long pool, about twenty yards wide, nowhere more than five feet deep, no strong hovers on either side the bank; but below us was dangerous ground. So a shallow was guarded by two of us, with our breeches rolled up and long sticks in our hands.

Well, we hunted our otter up and down that pool for two hours. He was given no rest; he came quietly to a corner where the water was shallow; Rally and her big puppy were there. They saw the round, brown head and bead-like eyes, and furiously rushed on to their game. What a row! What a fight! The terriers were there; all of us were there. Torn jackets and torn coats. It was a wonder that during the *melée* our otter did not escape and we ourselves be the bitten ones. How it all came about none of us well knew, but a quarter of an hour later, three lads, a man, and a fisherman, were sitting in a green meadow, where wild hyacinths made the hedgerows blue and the clover was imparting fragrance to the air. They were sitting there with their hounds and their terriers, and whilst the scratch pack rolled and dried themselves amongst the earlier summer flowers, we were gazing in astonishment at an otter weighing 25½lb.—one that we had killed ourselves with the aid of our two hounds and terriers. We had walked three miles to perform this feat, and, need I say, that in less than two years from that time that locality had as good a pack of otter hounds as man need desire. Our Mentor of the day was our huntsman.

Notwithstanding this experience of my own, almost all old hunters say that many years careful work are required to perfect a pack of otter hounds. Squire Lomax, of Clitheroe, over a quarter of a century ago, had the misfortune to lose his entire pack through an attack of dumb madness. Now his were perhaps the most accomplished lot of otter hounds any man ever possessed. Each hound was perfect in itself, and the pack might have found and killed an otter without the slightest assistance from their esteemed master, who had taken years to bring them to their state of perfection. "You will soon get another pack together, Mr. Lomax," said a friend. "No," was the reply, "my old hounds took me the best part of a lifetime to obtain, and should I recommence again, I should be an old man and past hunting, before I got another lot to my liking." Mr. Lomax for years hunted the Ribble, Lune, and other rivers in the north.

Mr. Gallon, of Bishop Auckland, who met his death whilst otter hunting in Scotland, was another great authority on this hound, and his opinion was pretty much the same as that of Mr. Lomax. But good sport can be had without having hounds quite so perfect as those mentioned.

I am, however, getting a little in advance of my text, and something must be said of the earlier days of the otter hound. King John is said to have had a pack, of which he was very fond. Although thus early otter hunting was considered royal sport, the otter was only placed in the third class of the beasts of the chase, ranking with the badger and the wild cat—even the timid hare and the hard-biting marten taking precedence. However, that he was highly valued, even in those days, for the amusement afforded, may be inferred from the fact that Edward II. (time 1307), had, as part of his household, a huntsman and subordinates to look after his otter hounds. Sometimes the King's otter hunter resided in the hall, and was served there; on other occasions he had his own residence, and lived as he liked. Anyhow, he had "twelve otter dogges" in his care, and in addition a couple of greyhounds. Then there were "two boys" to look after the hounds and feed them. The master of the otter hounds was, as the times went, fairly well rewarded for his duties, he receiving in addition to "a robe in cloth yearly, or a mark in money" —the latter 13s. 4d.—and an extra allowance of four shillings and eightpence for shoes, twopence per day wages. Each of the so-called "boys" was remunerated at the rate of three halfpence per day. The latter did not appear to have any perquisites (tips are a more modern institution), but they would doubtless reside in the house or at the kennels.

It would have been interesting to know as a certainty the class of hounds the above were, but there is little doubt they were hard in coat and rough in hair, much as they are at the present day. Some time later the otter hound appeared to become less fashionable. He was kept by the " tinkèrs," and similar class of roving individuals, on the northern borders. There were a few in Wales. Early in the present century they were not uncommon in the south of Scotland, in Devonshire and the west, and in the north of England. Since, the otter hound has become a greater favourite, and at the present time, during the season, which may be said to last from the middle of April to the end of September, some eighteen to twenty well regulated packs hunt the otter in various parts of the kingdom.

In a few cases, usually in Devonshire, foxhounds are almost entirely used; elsewhere the packs are composed of the rough-haired otter hound, with occasionally a couple or so of foxhounds to assist them. Still, each variety of the hound should stick to that game for which nature intended him, the foxhound to the fox, the harrier to the hare, the otter hound to the otter. The latter is mostly followed on foot, and the foxhound is too quick and fast, though many like him because of his dash. In the staidness and care of the otter hound lie his character, and he will give better sport in most cases at his own game than any other hound.

Some of the most noted packs of the present day are those of the Hawkstone, which originally belonged to the late Hon. Geoffrey Hill, who died in 1891. They ultimately passed into the hands of Mr. R. Carnaby Forster, who hunted them until 1895, when Mr. H. P. Wardell took the mastership, and who continues to show excellent sport. Mr. Hill, who hunted from Maesllwch Castle, in Radnorshire, had the pack from his brother, Lord Hill, in 1869, and from that time to the day of his death had improved it immensely. There were twenty-five couples in the kennels, all good-looking, handsome, rough hounds, perhaps not so perfect in this work as those of Mr. Lomax, but in "sortiness" they have never been equalled. They were well cared for; the members of the hunt had a handsome costume, and hounds were taken to and fro in a van made for the purpose. From 1870 to 1890 these hounds killed 704 otters, no fewer than sixty-two being accounted for in one season, the best on record that of 1881. In 1893 they killed forty-one otters in forty-eight hunting days, but if a pack kills from a dozen to two dozen otters during the four or five months they hunt, a bad record is not made, for sometimes when the waters are in flood, or the hay crop remains uncut, hounds may not be out for a week, or even a longer interval may intervene between one meet and another.

The Carlisle hounds are another noted lot, and, with a slight interval, during which Mr. James Steel was the master, that position was occupied by Mr. J. C. Carrick for over a quarter of a century, viz , until 1894, when Mr. G. A. Mounsey Heysham became master, and now, in 1897, he has the assistance of Mr. Carrick as secretary. For some time the Carlisle hounds were as invincible on the showbench as by the river. Then "the Kendal" sprang up in the sister county, and, with the late Mr. Wilson, of Dallam Tower, as master, Troughton as huntsman, and having extraordinary success in breeding young hounds, they won all before them in the ring. Afterwards the late Mr. W. Tattersall took these hounds in hand, hunting them until 1891, when they were sold as stated below. However, Sir Henry Bromley, who in 1895 came into the Dallam Tower estates, resuscitated the Kendal pack; and is hunting them at the present time, there being about twenty couples of hounds in the kennels.

The Kendal Ragman was particularly successful at stud—no one ever had a better hound at work, and he lasted eight seasons. He was a black and tan, rather short in coat to be quite right, but what there was had an extraordinary texture, so hard and close and crisp that I have seen the water standing in drops thereon, quite unable to penetrate the dense covering.. This hound it was I saw take the head of an otter right in its jaws as the game came up for a breather close to the bank upon which Ragman was standing. The otter was very nearly finished outright ; it would have quite killed any other animal, for the fangs of the hound had gone deeply through the bone of the skull, perhaps just missing what might have been a vital part. These Kendal hounds were sold for something like £200 to Mr. Carnaby Forster, of Tarporley, Cheshire, at the commencement of 1891, who incorporated them with the Hawkstone already alluded to. This was, perhaps, the cheapest pack of hounds ever sold ; there were about twelve couples, with some terriers, and I am pretty certain that, placed publicly in the market, £1000 would have been obtained for the lot.

Another old master of otter hounds is Mr. John Benson, of Cockermouth ; but half a dozen years ago his hounds were discontinued, and in their place came a subscription pack, of which Mr. Harry Clift, who has served a very long apprenticeship to the sport, was at the head. But more changes were brewing here, and at the present time Mr. H. P. Senhouse is master, and Mr. J. H. Jefferson is working and hunting secretary. Mr. F. Collier now hunts his late uncle's hounds, which are perhaps better known as the Culmstock. Mr. W. Collier, down Devonshire way, hunted the otter for over fifty years, and Mr. Cheriton in the west likewise, but both appear to have preferred the dash and go of the foxhound to the sedateness and care of the pure variety. Mr. W. C. Yates has had some good hounds in his time. I once saw the latter—Mr. T. Wilkinson, of Neasham Abbey, hunting the pack during an off season, when he had not one of his own—kill three otters in one day, in Lancashire. Mr. Yates latterly hunted in Ireland, but in 1896 he sold the whole of his pack to Sir Henry Bromley. The Squire of Neasham, after an idle season or two, again got together his favourite hounds, and is still hunting in the neighbourhood of Durham, and goes into Northumberland occasionally. The latter county once had a pack of its own, the property of Major Brown. In Scotland, Captain Clarke Kennedy, some years ago, kept otter hounds; so did Dr. Grant, of Knockgray; and the Duke of Athol and others, nor can the west country hounds of Mr. Trelawny's be omitted.

Of more recently established packs, there are the Dumfriesshire, with a popular master in Mr. J. Bell-Irving, and an equally popular huntsman in Mr. W. Davidson; Mr. Edmund Buckley's (Wales); The Rug, the Hon. C. H. Wynne, master; The Pembroke and Carmarthen, Mr John Evans, master; and the Bucks, Mr. W. F. E. Uthwatt, master; may be specially mentioned. There are also other otter hounds hunting in Devonshire, Somersetshire, Hampshire, Yorkshire, Carmarthenshire, Merionethshire, Brecknockshire, in county Wexford, and near Dublin. Captain Dawson (Otley, Yorkshire) kept a pack of otter hounds for some years, but sold them to Sir Henry Bromley, in 1894, because of the scarcity of otters in his locality. Then Sir Cecil Legard had a pack in Yorkshire, which he gave up about the same time for a similar reason, and his hounds went to Mr. Assheton Smith, of Vaynol Park, who only kept them a couple of seasons, when they were sold to Mr. John Evans, master of the Pembroke and Carmarthen Otter Hounds.

The dog otter hound should stand about 25 inches at shoulder, the bitch about 23 inches. The best and most favourite colours are the blue and white, though not so much mottled as the beagle, and a hard looking pepper and salt colour. Yellow and fawn, and yellow or fawn and white hounds are likewise good old colours, and, as I have said, black and tan is not amiss, with, maybe, white on the breast and feet; but black tan and white in patches is not nice on an otter hound, however gaudy it may be on others of the race. I have also seen one or two almost white hounds, but never one of the latter with the correct coat, which should be hard and crisp and close, as water and weather resisting as possible, and not too long. Often the long coats incline to an indication of silkiness in texture, which, however, is preferable to a soft, woolly jacket. In build an otter hound should be like a foxhound, strong, level, and well put together, stern carried gaily, feet close and particularly hard, and this is even more desirable than in a foxhound, as being one minute in the water and another on the hard rocks and stones tries the pads very much. A big foot is likely to increase the pace in swimming. The head must be long, jaws strong and powerful, eyes giving a certain sedate and intellectual appearance; they sometimes show the haw, which is no defect. Ears long and pendulous, close set, in order that the water may be kept from penetrating into some of the delicate internal parts. However, what an otter hound ought to be the illustration preceding this article will best inform the reader searching after information. A nice weight for a dog hound is from 60lb., to 75lb., and for a bitch about 10lb. less.

POINTS.

	Value.		Value.
Coat	20	Head and ears	20
Legs and feet...........	20	Back and loins	10
Hind quarters and stern	10	Shoulders	5
Neck and chest	10	Symmetry and colour	5
	60		40

Grand Total **100**.

(From *Modern Dogs*.)

THE HOUND (OTTERHOUND).

ORIGIN.—Nothing positive is known about it, but probably a cross of Welsh harrier, "Southern hound," and a terrier, though some say it is of bloodhound extraction. The breed is very old.

USES.—For hunting the otter and other water-animals.

SCALE OF POINTS, ETC.

	Value.		Value.
Skull	10	Legs and feet . .	10
Jaws	10	Coat	10
Eyes	5	Stern	5
Ears	10	Symmetry and strength	10
Chest and shoulders . .	15		
Body and loins . . .	15	Total . .	100

GENERAL APPEARANCE.—Always excepting coat, it much resembles the bloodhound ; it should be perfect in symmetry, strongly built, hard and enduring, with unfailing powers of scent and a natural antipathy to the game it is bred to pursue.

HEAD.—Large, broader in proportion than the bloodhound's; forehead high; muzzle a fair length, and nostrils wide. Ears long, thin, and pendulous, fringed with hair.

NECK.—Not naturally long, and looks shorter than it really is from the abundance of hair on it.

SHOULDERS.—Slope well.

LEGS AND FEET.—Legs straight, and feet a good size; compact.

BACK.—Strong and wide; ribs, and particularly the back ribs, well let down.

THIGHS.—Big and firm, and hocks well let down.

STERN.—Well and thickly covered with hair, and carried well up, but not curled.

COLORS are generally grizzle or sandy, with black and tan more or less clearly defined.

Group of Hounds of the Dumfrieshire Otter Hunt
(Beach Grove, Annan, Eng.)

THE OTTERHOUND

Origin.—Nothing is positively known of the origin of this breed, but it is probably a cross of the Welsh harrier, "Southern hound" and a terrier, though some say it is of Bloodhound extraction. The breed is, however, very old.

Uses.—For hunting the otter and other water animals.

*STANDARD.

General Appearance.—Always, excepting coat, it much resembles the Bloodhound; it should be perfect in symmetry, strongly built, hard and enduring, with unfailing powers of scent and a natural antipathy to the game it is bred to pursue.

Head.—Large, broader in proportion than the Bloodhound's; forehead high; muzzle of fair length and nostrils wide. Ears long, thin and pendulous and fringed with hair.

32

Neck.—Not naturally long and appears shorter than it really is, on account of the abundance of hair on it.

Shoulders.—Sloping.

Legs.—Straight, and feet of good size but compact.

Back and Thighs.—Back strong and wide; ribs and particularly the back ribs well let down; thighs big and firm, and hocks well down.

Stern.—Well and thickly covered with hair and carried well up, but not curled.

Colors.—These are generally grizzle or sandy, with black and tan more or less clearly defined.

SCALE OF POINTS.

Skull	10	Body and loins	15
Jaws	10	Legs and feet	10
Eyes	5	Coat	10
Ears	10	Stern	5
Chest and shoulders	15	Symmetry and strength	10

Total.. 100

COMMENTS.

Though the Otterhound is built on about the same lines as the English Foxhound, he nevertheless presents a much more workmanlike and hardy appearance, due in no small degree to his rough coat. As his name implies, he is used to hunt the otter, and in order to successfully perform his duties he must, first of all, be possessed of a long head, powerful jaws and good level teeth. In order that the olfactory organs may be developed to the highest degree, the nostrils should be wide. Though the standard does not call for it the ears should be carried close to the head, as such are desired in all water dogs. Heavy shoulders and crooked front legs are glaring faults, while feet that are not compact and furnished with very hard pads become almost useless toward the end of a long hunt in the water. The back and hind-quarters are faulty if they show the slightest sign of weakness, and a dog deficient in this respect should not be a candidate for high honors. The coat of the Otterhound is one of its most essential points, though the standard makes no allusion to it whatever. In order to protect the dog as much as possible from the water, it should be not only crisp, hard and close, but it should be absolutely free from all woolly semblance, as wool certainly is not an expeller of water. Nor should it be too long. In addition to the colors given in the standard, authorities on the breed name yellow and fawn, or yellow or fawn and white, and consider black, white and tan objectionable. They also give 25 in. as the proper height for dogs, and 23 in. for bitches, while in matter of weight they give 60 to 75 lbs. to the dogs, the bitches weighing about 10 lbs. less. As a rule the Otterhound is somewhat higher on the leg than the Foxhound. Good bone is an essential quality in this breed and should be insisted upon.

THE OTTER-HOUND

ALTHOUGH many writers describe the Otter-hound as a dog of mixed breed, all refer him back to the old Southern Hound, or the Bloodhound, for his origin, whatever crosses may have been resorted to for producing the dog we now recognise as the legitimate hound to pursue the "Fish-slicer." Blaine says he is the old Southern Hound crossed with the Water Spaniel, and that those with a dash of the Bulldog in them are the best; the Water Spaniel being supposed to supply the roughness of coat—for Water Spaniels of the eighteenth century were very different in coat, as in other points, from those dogs of to-day called by that name—and also to give or to increase the aptitude for swimming, whilst the Bulldog cross is supposed to have infused the necessary hardiness, courage, and tenacity.

Both Youatt and Richardson suppose him to be the result of a cross between the Southern Hound and the Rough Terrier, and by others the Rough Deerhound has been held to have had a share in the production of the Otter-hound. If, however, any such cross ever occurred, by either accident or design, it is so remote and slight as to be now quite swallowed up; and as a stream is lost in the immensely larger volume of the river to which it is a tributary, so has any infusion of alien blood been absorbed by the true old English hound blood of the genuine Otter-hound.

The hunting of the otter is one of our most ancient sports. Jesse, in his researches into the history of the dog, gives many interesting quotations from ancient documents showing the pursuit with hounds to have been a Royal pastime with many of our English kings. In July, 1212, the Sheriff of Somerset received commands from King John to "provide necessaries for Ralph, the otter-huntsman, and Godfrey, his fellow, with two men and two horses, and twelve Otter-hounds, as long as they find employment in capturing otters in your shire." And John, the otter-hunter to King Edward I., had twelve otter dogs under his charge. An annual payment, called "Kilgh Dourgon," was made in Wales for

34

the king's water dogs with which otters were hunted ; and James I., an ardent sportsman, had for his Master of Otter-hounds John Parry, to superintend the hunt, and provide for the king's diversion ; and so on, from reign to reign, otter-hunting has, with varying patronage and popularity, remained a British sport, there being fifteen or sixteen packs at the present time, and these spread over England, Wales, Scotland, and Ireland. Some of them, like the Carlisle, the Cheriton, and the Culmstock, are old-time packs.

Otter-hunting has become a most popular sport within the last few years, and the followers of a good pack are very numerous. Instead, too, of employing quite a scratch pack for the purpose, as was at one time not uncommon, we have either the Otter-hound pure and simple (that is, the dog described and figured here), or the same dog with a number of Foxhounds. According to Mr. E. Buckley, whose name is well known in connection with the sport of otter-hunting, one very often gets the best sport from hitting off the " drag " (*i.e.* scent) left by the otter who has been travelling the night before. He has had runs up to four miles, sometimes finding in a "holt" (or "earth"), and sometimes without reward. From the time when he is driven from his " wicker couch," contrived "within some hollow trunk, where ancient alders shade the deep, still pool," the mephitic otter gives his pursuers plenty to do, and when it comes to close quarters, be it with Terrier or with hound, makes, as opportunity offers, good use of his teeth. Traced by his spraints and seal, and unharboured from his kennel or couch, he finds hard work for men and dogs, as the latter follow him up from holt to holt, and pool to pool, and the huntsmen eagerly watch for his "vents," or "chain."

In recent times otter-hunting has been modified to suit different circumstances, and practices in vogue in one hunt are tabooed in another. The spear is discontinued, and the practice of tailing the otter—that is, rushing in on him when worn and pressed, seizing him by the tail, swinging him round in the presence of the hounds, to excite them, and finally throwing him among them—whilst treated as an act of prowess in some otter-hunting districts, is strictly forbidden in others.

"Whoa-Whoop," a writer in the *Field*, thus interestingly describes the pastime :—

" A pack of otter-hounds consists of from nine to fourteen couples, and the variation of their appearance, some being smooth coated and some rough, lends a peculiar contrast to the eye. Two, three, or more Terriers are also employed for the purpose of driving the otter from its holt, and of these rough-coated ones are preferred. The staff is contained in a huntsman—generally the Master— a couple of whips, and in many Hunts a 'follower,' as the field are termed, called the 'amateur whip,' one whom, by his enthusiasm and general knowledge of the craft, has shown himself to be a useful addition to the Hunt. As in most cases, this division of the chase has its own 'calls,' the principal of which are a 'solid mark,' when the pack strike the true line of the 'trail,' which is the term applying distinctly to the scent of an otter; 'bubble avent,' for the air-bubbles which break the surface of a pool, showing the line of the otter's passage as it travels up or down stream under water. 'Heu gaze' is the term used when it appears in view, and it is 'watched' when it makes its 'holt,' as those elaborate underground workings made in the bank of the river are termed, in which it sometimes passes its time during the day, after having eaten a hearty breakfast; and then the 'spur' is the name given to its footprint.

The meet is usually made at some well-known trysting-place, which, though not always near to a railway, yet generally there may be found conveyances that will carry one to the river. The time of appointment entirely depends on the length of the river to be hunted. Those of a short course necessarily must be hunted earlier than those whose length extends far into the country, the reason for this being that it has been found that those otters which frequent the less lengthy streams generally return to the estuaries into which they empty, and unless you are up betimes the hounds will only strike a trail which will soon show that the otter has gone beyond their reach. Those, however, which inhabit the longer rivers often betake themselves up some of the smaller tributaries, and, leaving these some distance away from the main stream, find shelter during the day in the woods which are sometimes to be found in the vicinity. When the time of appointment has elapsed, the pack, which had arrived at the river side some time previously and have been duly rested, are what is called 'cast off,' or 'put to water,' and while some feather along each bank of the river, others swim the stream until at length a hound, whose note is well known to the pack, lifts its voice in quack cadence once or twice, then suddenly becomes mute. But as the rest of the pack gather round, knowing full well that their companion has not spoken without good cause, again comes the sound of their voices, which, gathering in strength in a few seconds, breaks into a lovely volume of melody. Now onward and upward dash the whole pack until, maybe, they reach a long, deep pool, to which, though they may have driven the trail with a good head, yet, as they take the deep water, all becomes as silent as the grave. Nothing discouraged, however, they begin without any hesitation at once to search silently every root and nook, while the huntsman, whips, and followers at the same time are eagerly looking along the side of the bank, seeking for some sign of the otter's presence.

At length one of the searchers lifts his head, yet still in silence, to call the attention of the huntsman, who immediately hastens to the spot, where on his knees he carefully examines that to which his notice has been drawn, and, after a few moments, raising himself from his prostrate position, winds his horn merrily. Immediately the whole pack gathers to his side, and as they rise the bank a beautiful chorus fills the air, they having once more touched the trail, the sign that had been found being the 'spur' of the otter where it had left the river. Then the hunt proceeds in all its excitement, but the certainty of a kill is always as improbable as it is probable, and in this is the beauty of the chase.

Should, however, the luck be with the pack and the hunt terminate with a good kill, the huntsman brings the now dead otter on the bank, and here he carries out the offices attached to the matter. First the 'pads' (feet) are dismembered from the legs and the 'mask' (head) is severed from the body. Then the 'pole' (tail) is cut off at the root, and now the 'pelt' (skin) is stripped from the carcase, which is then cast as a reward among the longing and excited pack. These trophies are distributed among the field of followers, the ladies, who often grace an otter-hunt with their presence, receiving their full share."

A breed of dogs selected and kept to this game, even if originally of the identical stock of our modern Bloodhounds, would naturally diverge in some characteristics, and the wet-resisting coat, so necessary to a dog so much in the water, would be developed ; whereas, on the contrary, the treatment to which the companion Bloodhound is subjected tends to fine and soften his coat: or there may have been rough-coated hounds of the Bloodhound type from which the Otter-hound has sprung ; and, according to both Caius and Turberville, Bloodhounds were used for this sport. But whether either of these suppositions is correct or not, he is in shape and voice and style so truly a hound that one cannot think he is indebted to a strain of either Spaniel, Terrier, or Deer-hound blood for his rough and wet-resisting coat.

Mr. Buckley says : " I have tried a cross with the Bloodhound, but it was a failure, as the progeny were much too tender. I think the probable origin was the Southern Hound, Water Spaniel, and old Harrier blood. This, however, is only my individual opinion, derived from ten years' breeding ; but it is difficult to say, as there are at least two distinct types."

In general appearance—always excepting the coat—the Otter-hound much resembles the Bloodhound ; he should be perfect in symmetry, strongly built, hard and enduring, with unfailing powers of scent, and a natural antipathy to the game he is bred to pursue. The head should be large, broader in proportion than the Bloodhound's, the forehead high, the muzzle a fair length, and the nostrils wide ; the ears long, thin, and pendulous, fringed with hair ; the neck not naturally long, and looking shorter than it really is, from the abundance of hair on it. The shoulders should slope well, the legs be straight, and the feet a good size (with as much webbing between the toes as possible, as this assists him to swim), but compact ; the back strong and wide ; the ribs, and particularly the back ribs, well let down ; the thighs big and firm, and the hocks well let down ; the stern well and thickly covered with hair, and carried well up,

FIG. 47.—MR. E. BUCKLEY'S OTTER-HOUND MAWDDWY STANLEY.

but not curled. The colours are generally grizzle or sandy, with black and tan more or less clearly defined, or black and tan with a *slight* tinge of grizzle.

The Otter-hound is one of the few varieties of the Domestic dog that is puzzling to the novice. True, the breed is occasionally represented at shows in winter and late autumn ; but it is only at the more important gatherings, like those of the Kennel Club, Birmingham, and Cruft's, that a classification is provided. There one finds represented the Dumfriesshire packs, or those associated with the names of Mr. Uthwatt or Mr. Buckley. To the latter gentleman we are indebted for the following measurements and weight of a well-known show-bench winner and worker in his Mawddwy Stanley (fig. 47): Age, 4¾ years; weight, 90lb.; height at shoulders, 26in.; length from nose to set-on of tail, 45in.; length of tail, 17in.; girth of chest, 31in.; girth of loin, 27in.; girth of head, 19½in.; girth of fore arm, 7½in.; length of head from occiput to tip of nose, 11in.; girth of muzzle, midway between eyes and tip of nose, 11½in.; ear, 9in.

The Otterhound

Otter-hunting is a very ancient sport, otter dogs being used during the reign of King John.

The Hounds in those days had not the beauty of the present-day Otterhound, as very different types of dogs were then used, *e.g.*, a cross-bred Terrier, Foxhounds, etc.

One of the best packs of Otterhounds in this country are those belonging to the Dumfriesshire otter-hunt, the River Tweed affording the pack excellent hunting ground. It is an old-established pack, and has always given, we believe, the best of sport.

Looking at a typical specimen of this breed, one is not slow to recognise a "workman all over."

To a casual observer he has the appearance of a rough-coated—if such there can be—Bloodhound.

These dogs weigh from about 65 to 80 or 90 lbs., and the bitch Hounds 10 or 15 lbs. less, and of different colours, but grizzle (black and grey), and tan is the most general.

Colour.—Fawn, yellow, blue and white and black-

* The heights of the Crickhowell Harriers are as follows :—
Dogs, 17½ to 18½ inches ; bitches, 17 to 18 inches.

and-tan are frequently seen. The last-named colour should not be encouraged in these Hounds.

White markings are common.

His coat should be dense, of a wiry texture, shaggy in appearance, and of a water-resisting nature.

When judging these dogs, particular attention is paid to the coat.

A soft coat is decidedly objectionable, so is one that is thin.

Height.—About 25 inches.

Eyes.—Deeply sunk, thoughtful, showing the "haw" plainly.

Ears.—Long and sweeping, hanging closely to the cheeks.

Skull.—The peak is less prominent than that of the Bloodhound and the head shorter, but the flews large and loose. Like the ears, it is coverd by shaggy hair, softer than that on the body. Beneath the lower jaw there is a moustache. Large teeth and powerful jaws are indispensable in an encounter with an otter.

Of Foxhound-like conformation, the frame is of stouter build altogether.

Neck.—Thick, of medium length, ending in very powerful shoulders and arms, and the chest must be deep, running and swimming demanding a sound heart and lungs. Dewlap loose. A strong back and loins, the latter slightly arched, an additional qualification of the breed. Should be shorter in the leg than a Foxhound, but have big-boned, muscular limbs, with large feet, close, and horny below.

These Hounds hunt both by scent and by sight, their scenting-power being developed to a remarkable degree.

The music of Otterhounds is rich, deep and mellow.

THE OTTERHOUND.

BY GEORGE S. LOWE.

" My hounds are bred out of the Spartan kind,
So flew'd, so sanded ; and their heads are
hung
With ears that sweep away the morning dew ;
Crook-knee'd, and dew-lapp'd like Thessalian
bulls ;

Slow in pursuit, but match'd in mouth like
bells,
Each under each. A cry more tuneable
Was never halloo'd to, nor cheer'd with horn,
In Crete, in Sparta, nor in Thessaly :
Judge, when you hear."
—" A MIDSUMMER NIGHT'S DREAM."

THE Otterhound is a descendant of the old Southern Hound, and there is reason to believe that all hounds hunting their quarry by nose had a similar source. Why the breed was first called the Southern Hound, or when his use became practical in Great Britain, must be subjects of conjecture ; but that there was a hound good enough to hold a line for many hours is accredited in history that goes very far back into past centuries. The hound required three centuries ago even was all the better esteemed for being slow and unswerving on a line of scent, and in many parts of the Kingdom, up to within half that period, the so-called Southern Hound had been especially employed. In Devonshire and Wales the last sign of him in his purity was perhaps when Captain Hopwood hunted a small pack of hounds very similar in character on the fitch or pole-cat ; the *modus operandi* being to find the foraging grounds of the animal, and then on a line that might be two days old hunt him to his lair, often enough ten or twelve miles off.

When this sort of hunting disappeared, and improved ideas of fox-hunting came into vogue, there was nothing left for the Southern Hound to do but to hunt the otter. He may have done this before at various periods, but history rather tends to show that otter-hunting was originally associated with a mixed pack, and some of Sir Walter Scott's pages seem to indicate that the Dandie Dinmont and kindred Scottish terriers had a good deal to do with the sport. It is more than probable that the rough-coated terrier is identical with the now recognised Otterhound as an offshoot of the Southern Hound ; but be that as it may, there has been a special breed of Otterhound for the last eighty years, very carefully bred and gradually much improved in point of appearance. They are beautiful hounds to-day, with heads as typical as those of Bloodhounds, legs and feet that would do for Foxhounds, a unique coat of their own, and they are exactly suitable for hunting the otter, as everyone knows who has had the enjoyment of a day's sport on river or brook.

The very existence of the otter is a mystery. He seldom allows himself to be seen. There is a cunning about the animal that induces him to live far away from the haunts of man, and to occupy two totally different points of vantage, as it were, in as many hours. He may live in a burrow on a cliff by the sea, and his fishing exploits may extend seven or eight miles up a river, generally in the hours nearest midnight. A stream in South Devon defied whole generations of otter hunters, or perhaps, more properly speaking, the otters did. No matter how early in the morning the hunt was started, there would be a hot trail up stream, hounds throwing their tongues and dashing from bank to bank, through pools, over clitters of rocks, and often landing on meadow-side ; but there would be no otter, and then the hunt would turn and hounds would revel on a burning scent down stream, the quarry meanwhile sleeping in his sea-girt holt perfectly safe from any interference. Then, again, the otter may live on the moorside at the head of

the river, and fish down and back. He is then more accessible, and it is under such conditions that the best sport is obtained. But still these animals are wrapt in wondrous mystery. The Rev. C. Davies, who wrote in *The New Sporting Magazine* under the *nomme de guerre* of " Gelert," in giving his experience of South Devon otter-hunting early in the 'forties, relates that he

THE SOUTHERN HOUND (1803).

From " The Sportsman's Cabinet."   By P. Reinagle, R.A.

quite astonished old resident farmers when he first commenced hunting near their homesteads. They asked him what he was doing. He replied that he was " otterhunting," and they laughed, and told him they had never heard of such an animal ; and yet he must have killed over fifty in the next five years within a mile of them, and of course otters had always been there. It was the reverend gentleman's surmise, therefore, that the otter inhabits nearly every river in Great Britain, but that there is no knowing his whereabouts until he is regularly hunted.

There are different opinions on the subject as to how the otter should be hunted, and the kind of hound best suited for the sport. Mr. Davies leant towards the modern Foxhound, and he had many disciples holding the same views. They believed in the dash of the Foxhound to keep the otter moving as soon as he was dislodged from his holt, and it is certainly very grand to see a pack of Foxhounds swimming at really a great pace up stream and to hear their voices fairly echo amid the petty roar of waterfall or the bubbling of rapid stream. It is sport that can never be forgotten. Such was shown by Mr.

MR. J. C. CARRICK'S SWIMMER
BY LUCIFER—COUNTESS.
From a Painting by George Earl.

Davies, and later by Mr. Trelawny's hounds, the latter being the Master of the Dartmoor country at the time ; and in the summer he hunted otter with fourteen or fifteen couples of his Foxhounds, and about one couple of rough Otterhounds (Cardigan being a notable one), and of course two or three terriers. The old squire would never admit, however, that the regular Otterhound was as good as the Foxhound, which he would argue was better in every part of a hunt than Cardigan. Others differ partially from this view, and consider that Foxhounds will miss a good many otters in their over-anxiety to get forward.

The Otterhound proper is very steady and methodical ; he feels for a trail on boulder or rock, and if he touches it he will throw his tongue just once or twice. The scent may be one or two days old ; but if fresher he repeats his own challenge, becomes full of intent, moves a little up stream, crosses the river, back again perhaps, tells by his manner that the quarry is about ; and if the hound is a good one, and he is not hurried, he is sure to find, although it may be three or four miles from the starting point. Foxhounds might miss all this. The Otterhound, again, is the far better marker. The otter may be in some drain a couple of hundred yards away from the river, and his outlet may be at the root of some old trees washed by the constant flow into a deep refuge under water to the depth of possibly four or five feet. Foxhounds may flash over such a holt, but the experienced Otterhound is always on the look-out for such places. He steadies himself as he swims that way, turns his head to the bank, is not quite sure, so lifts himself to the trunk of the tree bending down to the water. The otter has landed there in the night, and a voice like thunder says so. It is a find. The pack will be all there now, and the notes of delight, becoming savage, concern the otter so far that he will generally shift his quarters at this stage without the aid of the terrier. The tell-tale chain of bubbles is then seen, or the animal coming up to vent, and then the hunt is in all its fullest excitement. He may beat them, by slipping down stream, or into very deep water ; but, with good hounds and the right sort of men as the hunters, the odds are against the otter.

There was one point upon which Squire Trelawny was very particular, and that was that the otter was not to be touched in any way, but left entirely to the hounds. If it came to his ears that one had been hit by a pole, nothing could well exceed his anger ; and this was in contrast to the old-fashioned ways of Scotland, of which there are pictures of the otter being held up on a barbed spear.

The Dartmoor was always a very fair hunt, and it is so now, although for many years since detached from the fox-hunting establishment. It was in the hands at first of the late Mr. Gage Hodge, of Glaze-brook House, and afterwards of Major Green and Mr. A. Pitman.

There were three other otter hunts in Devonshire, notably Mr. Cheriton's, Mr. Newton's, and Mr. Collier's. Mr. Cheriton hunted the pure-bred rough Otterhounds, and had some very good-looking ones. He started hunting the North Devon rivers about the year 1850, and continued to do so until early in the 'seventies ; but the pack still retains his name, and has now for its Master Mr. Arthur Blake Heineman. A late return gives from ten to fifteen couples of hounds ; about half pure Otterhounds and half Foxhounds. Mr. Newton's hunt became the Tetcot after that gentleman retired ; while on Major Green's retirement in 1902 the Dartmoor went into committee, and is so managed at present under the Mastership of Mr. A. J. Pitman, of the Manor House, Huish.

The greatest otter hunter of the last century may have been the Hon. Geoffrey Hill, a younger brother of the late Lord Hill. A powerful athlete of over six feet, Major Hill was an ideal sportsman in appearance, and he was noted for the long distances he would travel on foot with his hounds. They were mostly of the pure rough sort, not very big ; the dogs he reckoned at about 23½ inches, bitches 22 : beautiful Bloodhound type of heads, coats of thick, hard hair, big in ribs and bones, and good legs and feet. In seeing them at a meet it was noticeable that some were much shorter in their coats than others—not shorter, however, than the coat of an Irish Terrier. Possibly these may have been cross-bred. Something, however,

must be allowed for the exposure and hard work that falls to the lot of an Otterhound in respect to coat. The Hon. Geoffrey Hill's hounds were in perfect command : a wave of his hand was enough to bring them all to any point he wanted, and he was remarkably quiet. This may be essential, as the otter is particularly wary and very easily disturbed.

It was a narrow, but deep brook, and

CHAMPION TEAM OF THE DUMFRIESSHIRE OTTERHOUNDS, WITH MR. WILSON DAVIDSON, HON. HUNTSMAN.

hounds flew from side to side. They did not appear to miss an inch of ground ; everything was examined, and that an otter could be missed seemed impossible. Presently, as two streams met, there was a waving of sterns, a voice giving forth, and then another to swell into a big chorus in a few minutes, and the trail was found. They still hunted steadily. The otter might move now at any second ; but there was no certainty that he would, and the hounds were hanging on his trail, probably twelve hours old, as if glued to him. Major Hill said very little to them, but his experienced eye saw where the real scene of action lay : a bit of a swamp, where several streams united, and down in a gorge under some trees where some deep back-water had collected, looked the ideal place for an otter's holt. A hollow below proved that the wily one had slipped through ; but the hounds forced him back to the holt, and each stream was tried in turn, but his relentless followers showed him no mercy, and in three parts of an hour from the time he left the holt they pulled him down, a big dog otter.

Major Hill seldom exhibited his hounds. They were seen now and then at Birmingham ; but, hunting as hard as they did through Shropshire, Staffordshire, Cheshire, and into Wales, where they got their best water, there was not much time for showing. Their famous Master has been dead now many years, but his pack is still going, and shows great sport under the Mastership of Mr. H. P. Wardell, the kennels being at Ludlow Racecourse, Bromfield.

The leading pack in the Kingdom for the last sixty years, at any rate, has been the Carlisle when in the hands of Mr. J. C. Carrick, who was famous both for the sport he showed and for his breed of Otterhound, so well represented at all the important shows. Such hounds as Lottery, first at Birmingham some years back, and Lucifer were very typical specimens ; but of late years the entries of Otterhounds have not been very numerous at the great exhibitions, and this can well be explained by the fact that they are wanted in greater numbers for active service, there being many more packs than formerly—in all, twenty-one for the United Kingdom. Besides those already mentioned, there are, for instance, the Bucks, which hunt three days a week from Newport Pagnell on the rivers Ouse, Nene, Welland, Lovall, and Gleb ; Mr. T. Wilkinson's, at Darlington ; and the West Cumberland at Cockermouth. In Ireland there is the Brookfield, with its headquarters in County Cork ; while in Wales there are the Pembroke and Carmarthen, the Rug, the Ynysfor, and Mr. Buckley's.

The Crowhurst Otter Hunt hunts most of the rivers in Sussex with sixteen couples of hounds, including seven couples of pure Otterhounds. The " Master " last season was Mrs. Walter Cheesman. The Essex have, appropriately enough, their kennels at Water House Farm, Chelmsford. They hunt three days a week on the rivers of Essex and West Suffolk, with a pack of about eight couples of pure Otterhounds and a like number of Foxhounds. L. Rose, Esq., is the Master, and he hunts them himself. The Culmstock, with kennels now at Ilminster, is a very old hunt, established and maintained for over fifty years by Mr. William P. Collier, who hunted his own hounds, and showed great sport on the rivers in Somersetshire and North and East Devon. The Master at the present time is J. H. Wyley, Esq., and he carries the horn himself. Mr. Hastings Clay hunts a pack from Chepstow, and shows a good deal of sport on many of the Welsh rivers, as also in Gloucestershire and Herefordshire. Otter-hunting, really introduced into the New Forest by the Hon. Grantley Berkeley, is now continued in that district very successfully by Mr. Courtney Tracey, with about fifteen couples of pure and crossed hounds. The Northern Counties Hunt was established as recently as 1903, and up to the present the hounds have been drafts from the Culmstock, Hawkstone, Dumfriesshire, Mr. Thomas Robson's, and the Morpeth. They hunt the rivers over a very wide country, as they find their sport on the Tweed and the Tyne in Northumberland and go down to the Swale at Middleham, Yorkshire. Other packs have hunted these rivers in the past, such as those belonging to the well-known Mr. John Gallon, Major Browne—the great buyer of the Poltimore Foxhounds—and Mr. T. L. Wilkinson ; but they were not called the Northern Counties. They are now under the Mastership of F. P. Barnett, Esq., of Whalton, Newcastle-on-Tyne.

Another pack to hunt other Yorkshire waters, mostly in the West Riding districts, is the Wharfdale, with kennels at Addington. The present hunt was only established in 1905, but there had been a Wharfdale Otter Hunt Club, who invited certain

47

BREAKING COVER.

FROM THE PAINTING BY WALTER HUNT.

hunts to their rivers. Now the whole country is taken up, and that also which was formerly hunted by the famous Kendal Otterhounds. The pack at present comprises twenty couples. Mr. W. Thompson is the Master, and they hunt three days a week.

The two packs that appear to be most staunchly attached to the pure Otterhound are the Dumfriesshire and the East of Scotland. The former of these admits of nothing but sixteen couples of purebred Otterhounds. The hunt was established in 1889, but not with such hounds as are kennelled now by J. B. Bell Irvine, Esq., of Bankside, Lockerbie. They hunt all the rivers in the South of Scotland as far as those of Ayrshire, and by all accounts show excellent sport. It is evident that the Dumfriesshire, as hunted now by the very well-known sportsman, Mr. Wilson Davidson, are the typical Otterhounds shown between 1870 and 1880, by Mr. J. C. Carrick, the Hon. Geoffrey Hill, Mr. W. Tattersall, Mr. C. S. Coulson, and Mr. Forster. Mr. J. C. Carrick had three very good hounds in the 'seventies, called Booser, Stanley, and the bitch Charmer. The two last were immensely admired when they took first prizes in their respective classes at Birmingham in 1876. In the following year there were good classes at the Alexandra Palace, when one of Mr. Carrick's called Royal won. The mantle of Mr. J. C. Carrick has probably fallen on the Dumfriesshire, as in October, 1906, at the Crystal Palace show, the entries were confined to the kennel in question with one exception—Mr. J. H. Stocker's Dauntless Lady. The Dumfriesshire had two couples entered in the dog class—namely, Thunderer, Stormer, Bruiser, and Bachelor, all home-bred examples, and likewise the two bitches Thrifty and Darling, the first by Stanley out of Truthful, the other by the same sire out of Doubtful. The portrait on p. 154 is that of Swimmer, shown some years back by Mr. J. C. Carrick at Birmingham : the exact type of what the true-bred Otterhound should be. It is from an oil painting by George Earl.

The East of Scotland is a pack boasting of eleven couples of rough Otterhounds which was established in 1904. They hunt some of the rivers formerly belonging to the Dumfriesshire, or at least they were invited by the East Lothian Otter Hunt Club, which, with the half of the Berwickshire, started the East of Scotland pack. They hunt on no fixed days. The Master is W. M. Saunderson, Esq., of Crammond Bridge, Midlothian.

Enough has been said to show that the sport of otter-hunting is decidedly increasing, as there have been several hunts started within the last four years. There can well be many more, as, according to the opinion already quoted of that excellent authority, the late Rev. " Otter " Davies, as he was always called, there are otters on every river ; but, owing to the nocturnal and mysterious habits of the animals, their whereabouts or existence is seldom known, or even suspected. Hunting them is a very beautiful sport, and the question arises as to whether the pure Otterhounds should not be more generally used than they are at present. It is often asserted that their continued exposure to water has caused a good deal of rheumatism in the breed, that they show age sooner than others, and that the puppies are difficult to rear. There are, however, many advantages in having a pure breed, and there is much to say for the perfect work of the Otterhound The scent of the otter is possibly the sweetest of all trails left by animals. One cannot understand how it is that an animal swimming two or three feet from the bottom of a river bed and the same from the surface should leave a clean line of burning scent that may remain for twelve or eighteen hours. The supposition must be that the scent from the animal at first descends and is then always rising. At any rate, the oldest Foxhound or Harrier that has never touched otter is at once in ravishing excitement on it, and all dogs will hunt it. The terrier is never keener than when he hits on such a line.

The Foxhound, so wonderful in his forward dash, may have too much of it for otter-hunting. The otter is so wary. His holt can very well be passed, his delicious scent may be over-run ; but the pure-bred Otterhound is equal to all occasions. He is terribly certain on the trail when he finds it. Nothing can throw him off it, and when his deep note swells into a sort of savage howl, as he lifts his head towards the roots of some old pollard, there is a meaning in it—no mistake has been made. In every part of a run it is the same ; the otter dodges up stream and down, lands for a moment, returns to his holt ; but his adversaries are always with him, and as one sees their steady work the impression becomes stronger and stronger that for the real sport of otter-hunting there is nothing so good as the pure-bred Otterhound. There is something so dignified and noble about the hound of unsullied strain that if you once see a good one you will not soon forget him. He is a large hound, as he well needs to be, for the "var-mint" who is his customary quarry is the wildest, most vicious, and, for its size, the most powerful of all British wild animals, the inveterate poacher of our salmon streams, and consequently to be mercilessly slaughtered, although always in sporting fashion. To be equal to such prey, the hound must have a Bulldog's courage, a Newfoundland's strength in water, a Pointer's nose, a Retriever's sagacity, the stamina of the Foxhound, the patience of a Beagle, the intelligence of a Collie.

THE PERFECT OTTERHOUND.

1. **Head.**—The head, which has been described as something between that of a Bloodhound and that of a Foxhound, is more hard and rugged than either. With a narrow forehead, ascending to a moderate peak.

2. **Ears.**—The ears are long and sweeping, but not feathered down to the tips, set low and lying flat to the cheeks.

3. **Eyes.**—The eyes are large, dark and deeply set, having a peculiarly thoughtful expression. They show a considerable amount of the haw.

4. **Nose.**—The nose is large and well developed, the nostrils expanding.

5. **Muzzle.**—The muzzle well protected with wiry hair. The jaw very powerful with deep flews.

DOG HOUNDS OF THE DUMFRIESSHIRE OTTER HUNT, INCLUDING THUNDER AND SPANKER, ATTENDED BY THE WHIP'S DAUGHTER.

6. **Neck.**—The neck is strong and muscular, but rather long. The dewlap is loose and folded.

7. **Chest.**—The chest, deep and capacious, but not too wide.

8. **Back.**—The back is strong, wide and arched.

9. **Shoulders.**—The shoulders ought to be sloping, the arms and thighs substantial and muscular.

10. **Feet.**—The feet, fairly large and spreading, with firm pads and strong nails to resist sharp rocks.

11. **Stern.**—The stern when the hound is at work is carried gaily, like that of a rough Welsh Harrier. It is thick and well covered, to serve as a rudder.

12. **Coat.**—The coat is wiry, hard, long and close at the roots, impervious to water.

13. **Colour.**—Grey, or buff, or yellowish, or black, or rufus red, mixed with black or grey.

14. **Height.**—22 to 24 inches.

THE OTTERHOUND

THE Otterhound is a descendant of the old Southern Hound, and there is reason to believe that all hounds hunting their quarry by nose had a similar source. Why the breed was first called the Southern Hound, or when his use became practical in Great Britain, must be subjects of conjecture ; but that there was a hound good enough to hold a line for many hours is accredited in history that goes very far back into past centuries. The hound required three centuries ago even was all the better esteemed for being slow and unswerving on a line of scent, and in many parts of the Kingdom, up to within half that period, the so-called Southern Hound had been especially employed. In Devonshire and Wales the last sign of him in his purity was perhaps when Captain Hopwood hunted a small pack of hounds very similar in character on the fitch or pole-cat ; the *modus operandi* being to find the foraging grounds of the animal, and then on a line that might be two days old hunt him to his lair, often enough ten or twelve miles off.

When this sort of hunting disappeared, and improved ideas of fox-hunting came into vogue, there was nothing left for the Southern Hound to do but to hunt the otter. He may have done this before at various periods, but history rather tends to show that otter-hunting was originally associated with a mixed pack, and some of Sir Walter Scott's pages seem to indicate that the Dandie Dinmont and kindred Scottish terriers had a good deal to do with the sport. It is more than probable that the rough-coated terrier is identical with the now recognised Otterhound as an offshoot of the Southern Hound ; but be that as it may, there has been a special breed of Otterhound for the last eighty years, very carefully bred and gradually much improved in point of appearance. They are beautiful hounds to-day, with heads as typical as those of Bloodhounds, legs and feet that would do for Foxhounds, a unique coat of their own, and they are exactly suitable for hunting the otter, as everyone knows who has had the enjoyment of a day's sport on river or brook.

The greatest otter hunter of the last century may have been the Hon. Geoffrey Hill, a younger brother of the late Lord Hill. A powerful athlete of over six feet, Major Hill was an ideal sportsman in appearance, and he was noted for the long distances he would travel on foot with his hounds. They were mostly of the pure rough sort, not very big ; the dogs he reckoned at about 23½ inches, bitches 22 : beautiful Bloodhound type of heads, coats of thick, hard hair, big in ribs and bones, and good legs and feet.

Major Hill seldom exhibited his hounds. They were seen now and then at Birmingham ; but, hunting as hard as they did through Shropshire, Staffordshire, Cheshire, and into Wales, where they got their best water, there was not much time for showing. Their famous Master has been dead now many years, but his pack is still going, and shows great sport as the Hawkstone under the Mastership of Mr. H. P. Wardell, the kennels being at Ludlow race-course, Bromfield.

The leading pack in the Kingdom for the last sixty years, at any rate, has been the Carlisle when in the hands of Mr. J. C. Carrick, who was famous both for the sport he showed and for his breed of Otterhound, so well represented at all the important shows. Such hounds as Lottery and Lucifer were very typical specimens ; but of late years the entries of Otterhounds have not been very numerous at the great exhibitions, and this can well be explained by the fact that they are wanted in greater numbers for active service, there being many more packs than formerly—in all, twenty-one for the United Kingdom.

The sport of otter-hunting is decidedly increasing, as there have been several hunts started within the last six years. There can well be many more, as, according to the opinion of that excellent authority, the late Rev. " Otter " Davies, as he was always called, there are otters on every river ; but, owing to the nocturnal and mysterious habits of the animals, their whereabouts or existence is seldom known, or even suspected. Hunting them is a very beautiful sport, and the question arises as to whether the pure Otterhounds should not be more generally used than they are at present. It is often asserted that their continued exposure to water has caused a good deal of rheumatism in the breed, that they show age sooner than others, and that the puppies are difficult to rear. There are, however, many advantages in having a pure breed, and there is much to say for the perfect work of the Otterhound. The scent of the otter is possibly the sweetest of all trails left by animals. One cannot understand how it is that an animal swimming two or three feet from the bottom of a river-bed and the same from the surface should leave a clean line of burning scent that may remain for twelve or eighteen hours. The supposition must be that the scent from the animal at first descends and is then always rising. At any rate, the oldest Foxhound or Harrier that has never touched otter is at once in ravishing excitement on it, and all dogs will hunt it. The terrier is never keener than when he hits on such a line.

The Foxhound, so wonderful in his forward dash, may have too much of it for otter hunting. The otter is so wary. His holt can very well be passed, his delicious scent may be overrun ; but the pure-bred Otterhound is equal to all occasions. He is terribly certain on the trail when he finds it. Nothing can throw him off it, and when his deep note swells into a sort of savage howl, as he lifts his head towards the roots of some old pollard, there is a meaning in it—no mistake has been made. In every part of a run it is the same ; the otter dodges up stream and down, lands for a moment, returns to his holt ; but his adversaries are always with him, and as one sees their steady work the impression becomes stronger and stronger that for the real sport of otter-hunting there is nothing as good as the pure-bred Otterhound. There is something so dignified and noble about the hound of unsullied strain that if you once see a good one you will not soon forget him. He is a large hound, as he well needs to be, for the " varmint " who is his customary quarry is the wildest, most vicious, and, for its size, the most powerful of all British wild animals, the inveterate poacher of our salmon streams, and consequently to be mercilessly slaughtered, although always in sporting fashion. To be equal to such prey, the hound must have a Bulldog's courage, a Newfoundland's strength in water, a Pointer's nose, a Retriever's sagacity, the stamina of the Foxhound, the patience of a Beagle, the intelligence of a Collie.

THE PERFECT OTTERHOUND : Head—The head, which has been described as something between that of a Bloodhound and that of a Foxhound, is more hard and rugged than either. With a narrow forehead, ascending to a moderate peak. **Ears**—The ears are long and sweeping, but not feathered down to the tips, set low and lying flat to the cheeks. **Eyes**—The eyes are large, dark and deeply set, having a peculiarly thoughtful expression. They show a considerable amount of the haw. **Nose**—The nose is large and well developed, the nostrils expanding. **Muzzle**—The muzzle well protected from wiry hair. The jaw very powerful with deep flews. **Neck**—The neck is strong and muscular, but rather long. The dewlap is loose and folded. **Chest**—The chest, deep and capacious, but not too wide. **Back**—The back is strong, wide and arched. **Shoulders**—The shoulders ought to be sloping, the arms and thighs substantial and muscular. **Feet**—The feet, fairly large and spreading, with firm pads and strong nails to resist sharp rocks. **Stern**—The stern when the hound is at work is carried gaily, like that of a rough Welsh Harrier. It is thick and well covered, to serve as a rudder. **Coat**—The coat is wiry, hard, long and close at the roots, impervious to water. **Colour**—Grey, or buff, or yellowish, or black, or rufus red, mixed with black or grey. **Height**—22 to 24 inches.

OTTERHOUNDS.

IT has been said that the Otterhound is a cross between the Welsh Harrier, the Southern Hound and the Terrier. But there is every reason to think that the Bloodhound has been used in the evolution. In this connection the late Mr. Rawdon B. Lee in *Modern Dogs* says:—" The black-and-tan colour often appears in some strains (of Otterhounds), and his voice in many cases resembles the full, luscious tones of the Bloodhound more than the keener ring of the Foxhound. Prior to the outbreak of the Franco-German war, Count de Canteleu sent a number of French griffons to the late Mr. Waldron Hill, who then hunted from near Haddington, N.B. It was said that these importations, or some of them, were a direct cross with the wolf, and they and their progeny, bred with the Carlisle and Dr. Grant's hounds, were remarkably ferocious and keen. However, it is uncertain what eventually became of them, although it has been said they went back to France in 1871. Some years ago, Mr. J. C. Carrick, of Carlisle, was desirous of getting a fresh cross into his pack, and, with that intention, obtained a hound from the Western States of America. It was without pedigree, but resembled the Southern hound in Youatt's book. This Virginian importation, although not used at stud, did good duty on the show bench in the variety classes instead of improving a breed which was then quite as free from taint as any other variety of the modern dog. Much later Colonel Joynson imported a hound called Frivole, a wire-haired griffon of the Vendéen strain, which he used, in connection with the Dumfriesshire Otterhounds, with which his brother was connected, with considerable success, the dog Boatman, already alluded to, being one of her progeny. In appearance he much resembles an Otterhound with a somewhat short coat. There are many strains of these French long coated hounds which might be used to advantage so far as introducing new blood is concerned."

Illustrations of both "Frivole" and "Boatman" will be found on page 254; and the Southern Hound is depicted on page 242].

The remarks of Mr. George S. Lowe, in the *New Book of the Dog*, should also be recorded. That authority writes :—" The Otterhound is a descendant of the old Southern Hound, and there is reason to believe that all hounds hunting their quarry by nose had a similar source. Why the breed was first called the Southern Hound, or when his use became practical in Great Britain, must be subjects of conjecture ; but that there was a hound good enough to hold a line for many hours is accredited in history that goes very far back into past centuries. The hound required three centuries ago even was all the better esteemed for being slow and unswerving on a line of scent, and in many parts of the Kingdom, up to within half that period, the so-called Southern Hound had been especially employed. In Devonshire and Wales the last sign of him in his purity was perhaps when Captain Hopwood hunted a small pack of hounds very similar in character on the fitch or pole-cat ; the *modus operandi* being to find the foraging grounds of the animal, and then on a line that might be two days old hunt him to his lair, often enough ten or twelve miles off.

When this sort of hunting disappeared, and improved ideas of fox-hunting came into vogue, there was nothing

left for the Southern Hound to do but to hunt the otter. He may have done this before at various periods, but history rather tends to show that otter-hunting was originally associated with a mixed pack, and some of Sir Walter Scott's pages seem to indicate that the Dandie Dinmont and kindred Scottish terriers had a good deal to do with the sport. It is more than probable that the rough-coated terrier is identical with the now recognised Otterhound as an offshoot of the Southern Hound; but be that as it may, there has been a special breed of Otterhound for the last eighty years, very carefully bred and gradually much improved in point of appearance. They are beautiful hounds to-day, with heads as typical as those of Bloodhounds, legs and feet that would do for Foxhounds, a unique coat of their own, and they are exactly suitable for hunting the otter, as everyone knows who has had the enjoyment of a day's sport on river or brook."

However evolved, the Otterhound is here to-day, and affords the best of all sport. The nets and spears once used in the kill are now abolished and the hounds are able, with very little assistance, to kill their otter unaided.

Otter-hunting has been one of the Royal sports from an early date, both King John and Henry VIII. having kept packs.

There is no doubt that to perfect a pack of Otterhounds takes several years. Mr. Lomax, of Clitheroe, owned, about thirty-five years ago, probably the most accomplished pack that has ever been got together. "Each hound was perfect in itself, and the pack might have found and killed an otter without the slightest assistance from their esteemed and notable Master, who had taken years to bring them to their state of perfection." An outbreak of rabies resulted in the loss of the entire pack, save three hounds and several terriers. "You will soon get another pack together, Mr. Lomax," said a friend. "No," was the reply, "my old hounds took me the best part of a lifetime to obtain, and should I recommence again, I should be an old man and past hunting before I got another lot to my liking."

One of the greatest otter hunters of the last century was the Hon. Geoffrey Hill, a brother of the late Lord Hill, from whom he had his pack—the Hawkstone, one of the most noted packs to-day, the Master of which is Mr. H. P. Wardell. The Hon. Geoffrey Hill had his hounds in perfect command, a wave of his hand being sufficient to bring them to any point he wanted. From 1870 to 1890 these hounds killed 704 otters. In 1893 they killed 41 otters in forty-eight hunting days, and in 1902 they found 68 otters during sixty-four days' hunting and killed 53. Major Hill's hounds were occasionally exhibited at Birmingham, but the hard hunting they did left little time for showing.

Another noted pack is the Carlisle, of which Mr. J. C. Carrick was Master for over twenty-five years. These hounds were famous not only at their legitimate work but also on the show benches. Amongst other packs recently established there may be mentioned the Dumfriesshire, with Mr. J. Bell-Irving as Master; the Bucks; Mr. Hasting Clay's; the Essex; the East of Scotland; the Northern Counties; Mr. Courtenay Tracy's; the Cravenhurst; Mr. Hayne's; and the Wharfedale.

Otter-hunting, once decidedly on the wane, is now more popular than ever and the sport is distinctly increasing in favour. Hunting otters is a very beautiful sport. The scent of the otter is perhaps the sweetest of all, and all dogs will hunt it. In considering the type and size of hound to be bred for one must bear in mind the nature and character of the quarry, which is one of the wildest, most vicious and, for its size, the most powerful of our wild animals. "To be equal to such a prey," remarks Mr. George S. Lowe, "the hound must have a Bulldog's courage, a Newfoundland's strength in water, a Pointer's nose, a Retriever's sagacity, the stamina of the Foxhound, the patience of a Beagle, and the intelligence of a Collie."

THERE are numerous packs of Otter-hounds kept throughout the United Kingdom, but only in localities where rivers are well stocked with fish and where there is plenty of cover for the quarry of these dogs, *i.e.*, the otter. In some packs pure-bred Otter-hounds are kept, whereas others are of a mixed or nondescript variety. The typical hound is a very workmanlike animal, and seems to have been bred upon lines combining three essential qualities, viz., endurance, speed and adaptability to work of an aquatic nature. As to how the original type of Foxhound has been bred there does not appear to be any very reliable data, but it is a breed that is strongly suggestive of having been evolved from the old Southern hound, and probably the Bloodhound also. In all probability there are not more than two or three packs of pure Otter-hounds, but the Dumfriesshire pack consists of pure Otter-hounds. Many Otter-hound packs are composed of pure Foxhounds, Welsh hounds, or a cross between Foxhounds and pure Otter-hounds, and most masters of Otter-hounds are in favour of having a mixed

MEMBERS OF THE DUMFRIESSHIRE PACK

HOUNDS

To face page 148

61

pack, so that the latter can hunt on land for a prolonged period, for which work the pure Foxhound is the best; but if there is to be a long hunt on the banks, or in the water, either the cross-bred or the Otter-hound proves the best for such purposes. Many experienced huntsmen argue that the best hounds for otter-hunting are the pure-bred ones, but there are others, as previously stated, whose opinions are diametrically opposed to this view. A writer in the *Sporting and Dramatic News*, in giving expression to Mr William Littleworth's views (the Master of the Cheriton Pack), says: "My hounds are all smooth, Fox and Staghounds. In my opinion hounds ought not to speak without something to speak for. I am of opinion if you take a Foxhound young he can be trained to hunt anything, and almost every hound has a different method of working. My chief objection to the rough hounds is that they are too noisy. Some authorities argue that they stand the water better than the smooth hounds, but this must depend upon the texture of their coats, and from what I have seen they are more delicate than the Foxhound, which seems to me to have a hardier constitution. The only thing I can say in favour of the rough hounds is that they add to the tone of the music." Again, Mr Cameron's theories as to the utility of both classes of hounds are expressed in the following words: " If the Otterhound speaks more freely to an older drag the Fox-hound will slip away ' mute ' with an otter and spoil a day's sport. If the Otter-hound is not so quick at a kill, he is not so liable to ' riot,' especially at foxes, which are often found in osier beds when drawing for an otter. There are drawbacks on either side of the argument as to whether rough or smooth hounds should be employed. For looks and cry and all-round working qualities a pack of pure Otter-hounds is undoubtedly to be chosen; for a quick method of hunting, and for dash and finish at a kill, probably a mixed pack would be awarded the palm."

The same writer, in quoting the remarks of Mr C. H. Jefferson, the Master of the West Cumberland Foxhounds and the West Cumberland Otter-hounds, says that his preference is for a rough hound—half Foxhound and half Otter-hound. " I prefer this class to the pure Otter-hound; they are hardier in coat and hardier by nature, and, at the same time, maintain the rough appearance which Otter-hounds ought to have. There is no better hound for all-round work than the old seasoned Foxhound, which has become too slow for fox, but which, in his day, has been one of the best. I find these hounds take to hunting otters very quickly, and at present I have two in my pack which are splendid workers. I have only three pure-bred Otter-hounds, but I find

OTTER-HUNTING

HOUNDS

they cannot stand the hard work so well as the half-bred hound. For actually killing otters, and for quick, smart work, I would recommend a pack of old seasoned Foxhounds as I have referred to; but this would do away with the rough hound with its deep cry, which, in my opinion, adds so much to the pleasure of otter-hunting. At present I am breeding from, amongst others, a smooth black-and-tan bitch of Welsh blood, and crossed with a pure Otter-hound. She has bred me for the past three years some of the finest hounds, and this is the class of hounds I advocate—rough, hardy and active, with two or three old seasoned Foxhounds, which are most useful in any pack, though I unhesitatingly admit that from a spectacular point of view a pack of pure-bred hounds, such as the Dumfriesshire or Bucks, are far ahead of a mixed pack; but looks, in my opinion, are not everything, and, at any rate in my country, I have other things to consider."

Mr A. Jones, the Master of the Worcestershire Foxhounds and the Northern Counties Otter-hounds, expresses his views as follows: " I consider you must have a few pure-bred Otter-hounds in the pack, and the rest should comprise hounds bred from a pure Otter-hound bitch and the best working and looking Foxhound dog you can procure. Hounds bred in this way are much hardier, much quicker, have more drive, and their coats are much sooner dried than the pure-bred Otter-hound. The more stagnant the water the more useful the Otter-hound, but where rivers run fast, and are rocky and wide, you cannot do better than work the hounds I have described."

According to the foregoing authorities the introduction of the Foxhound cross is a benefit, and the product is a rough-coated hound, with Foxhound characteristics well in evidence. The crossing of a broken-coated variety of hound with a smooth-coated one ranks parallel with the common practice adopted by many Fox-terrier breeders, viz., mating a smooth Fox-terrier with a wire-haired one. The picture presented by a pack of pure Otter-hounds and that of an Otter and Foxhound crossed pack is as dissimilar as it is lacking in picturesqueness, but for quaintness and oddities the last named certainly take the palm. A typical Otter-hound will weigh from 80 lbs. to 100 lbs. or more, and measure about 26 inches at the shoulder. The skin should be thick and the hair of a grizzle colour. A deep chest, big-boned fore and hind limbs, strong loins and quarters, together with a stout neck and a back of medium length, are desirable qualities in these hounds. The head is rather narrow, the ears carried close to the sides of the head, the nostrils broad, the flews deep, and the eyes sunken, showing " haw." The facial expression and general appearance of these hounds is that of a powerfully-made, keen-looking dog, with

THE DUMFRIESSHIRE PACK

HOUNDS

To face page 152

a coat admirably adapted for water resistance. The constitution of the Otter-hound is usually of the most robust order, so that it is not the difficulty that is experienced in rearing puppies that renders the breeding of pure hounds so little practised. There has really no standard of points ever been laid down for Otter-hounds, and the sooner there is a clearly-defined code of such points formulated the better for the future welfare of the pure-bred Otter-hound. Once fixity of type is assured there ought not to be much trouble experienced in breeding Otter-hounds up to a constant standard of excellence.

The following are some of the principal packs of Otter-hounds in the United Kingdom:

BORDER COUNTIES, NORTH WALES

This is a subscription pack, and consists of thirty couples of mixed hounds. It hunts seven days a fortnight on the rivers Severn, Dovey, Banw, Conway, Ledr, Dysynni, Vyrnwy, Tanat, and tributaries in the counties of Merionethshire and Montgomery. In all these streams otters are frequently found, and good sport commonly enjoyed.

CARLISLE

This pack of hounds comprises twelve couples, and the kennel is at Carlisle. It is an old pack of Otter-hounds and hunts the rivers Eden, Esk, Petteril and Calgal, in which otters are tolerably numerous. It is a subscription pack with a minimum subscription of 2s. 6d.

The Cheriton

The Cheriton pack of Otter-hounds is composed of twelve couples of Fox and Staghounds, and was established about 1850 by Mr William Cheriton of Ellicombe, North Devon, who originally hunted both hares and otters with the pack, which hunts the rivers Teign, Little Dart, Taw, Toridge, Bray, Creedy, Yeo, Mole and Dalch. The waters are liable to sudden flood, and some of them are rapid streams. If it is a good season, as many as twenty otters will be killed.

Bucks

This pack consists of eighteen couples of pure Otterhounds, and hunts the following rivers: Stour, Ouse, Welland, Ivel, Cherwell, Sowe, Bain, Awn, Anker, Blythe, Lovatt, Nene, Granta, Evenlode, Wreake, Bowbrook, Windrush and tributaries, in the counties of **Bucks**, Beds, Hants, Warwick, Lincoln, Oxford, Rutland **and** some adjacent counties.

This is a subscription pack, and as the otters are fairly numerous, good sport is afforded.

Culmstock

The Culmstock pack consists of twenty couples of mixed hounds, and hunts the rivers Tone, Otter, Axe, Exex, Barle, Yeo, Yarty and tributaries. About thirty otters are usually killed in the season.

This is a subscription pack, and was established in 1837.

West Cumberland

The West Cumberland Otter-hounds is a mixed pack, consisting of twelve couples of cross-bred Foxhounds and Otter-hounds, and two couples of pure English Foxhounds. It is a very old pack and situated in a typical

HOUNDS

PURE OTTERHOUNDS AND FOXHOUNDS CROSSED WITH OTTERHOUNDS

70

otter-hunting country, the water in the streams being clear, and alternately deep and shallow. The following rivers are hunted by the pack: Derwent, Ellen, Dudden, Esk, Calder, Irt, Mite, along with various other streams in connection with lakes.

Mr Hasting Clay's

This pack meets on Tuesdays and Fridays, and comprises from twelve to fifteen couples of cross-bred hounds and Foxhounds. It hunts the rivers Wye, Usk, Trothy, Ely, Monnow, Ledden, Olway and Cowbridge, situated in the counties of Monmouth, Glamorgan, Hereford and Gloucester. The kennels are situated at Chepstowe, and the pack is a subscription one.

Dartmoor

The Dartmoor Otter-hounds were established in 1825, and since that time the pack has been under the mastership of about seven or eight gentlemen. The kennels are situated at South Brent, and the hounds generally meet about twice a week. It is composed of some fifteen couples, both Foxhounds and pure-bred hounds. It hunts the Dart, Avon, the Plym, Erme, Yealm, Harbourne, together with their tributaries, and sport is considered to be good.

Crowhurst

This is a subscription pack of Otter-hounds, consisting of sixteen couples, five or six couples of which are pure-bred Otter-hounds. The hounds meet two or three days a week, and hunt the following streams, in which otters are numerous: the Mole in Surrey, Kent and Sussex, the Rother in East and West Sussex, the Eden, Stour, Rover, Darenth, Medway, Rudwell, together with their tributaries. It is a subscription pack (minimum, £1, 1s.), and meets on Wednesdays and Saturdays. This hunt, being close to London, is a favourite one.

ESSEX

A subscription pack meeting three days a week, and composed of sixteen couples of hounds, one half being Foxhounds and the other half Otter-hounds. The rivers of Essex and Suffolk, likewise Herts, Cambs and Norfolk, are hunted by this pack, and very good sport is obtained, although the rivers are difficult to hunt, being slow, deep and overgrown with rushes in many parts.

Mr DAVID DAVIES's HOUNDS

These hounds are the property of the Master, and comprise sixteen couples, some pure Otter-hounds, but the majority Foxhounds. It hunts the upper portions of the Severn, Wye and Ellen, as well as other places.

EAST OF SCOTLAND OTTER-HOUNDS

The kennels of these hounds are close to Haddington, and the pack comprises eleven couples of rough Otter-hounds. It hunts the following rivers: Tweed, Tyne, Blackadder, Whiteadder, South Esk, Eden, Orr, Soltan, and many other rivers in which otters are numerous. It was established in 1904 and subscriptions received.

DUMFRIESSHIRE

The kennels of this pack are at Annan, the hounds of which hunt all rivers in the south of Scotland up to Ayrshire, there being about fourteen otters killed in a season. It is a subscription pack, consisting of sixteen couples of pure-bred Otter-hounds, and was established in 1889 by Mr W. Davison, assisted by others. The hounds

A FAMOUS OTTERHOUND, "TALISMAN"

To face page 156

from this kennel are practically the only ones shown at the Kennel Club Show in London, but it would be better if other masters with pure-bred Otter-hounds in their kennels would follow suit.

WHARFDALE

This pack was established in 1903 for hunting the Wharf and various other districts in that dale. This pack has its kennels at Giggleswick, Yorks, and meets three days a week, hunting the rivers Derwent, Esk, Aire, Nidd, also the Loone and Windermere Lake, together with the tributaries of the rivers in and around the locality.

NORTHERN COUNTIES

This is a mixed pack of hounds with the kennels close to Morpeth, comprising about sixteen couples of mixed hounds, which hunt the rivers Tweed, Tees, Swale, Tyne, North Tyne, Till, Glen, Wansbeck, Ure, etc., in Northumberland, Durham and part of Yorks, otters being numerous.

Mr COURTNEY TRACY'S

This subscription pack was established in 1887, and hunts the rivers Way and Till at Farnham, Meon and Itchin in the New Forest, the Nadder, Avon and Wylye in Wiltshire, together with the tributaries of the Stour, Dorsetshire, and various other streams.

THE YNYSFOR

These Otter-hounds hunt the rivers of Carnarvonshire, Anglesey, and a portion of those in Merionethshire. The hounds meet two days a week, being the property of the Master, whose ancestors established the pack over

74

a century since. It is composed of ten couples of Welsh Foxhounds, with the addition of a few pure-bred Foxhounds.

TETCOTT

This is a subscription pack and the kennels are at Bovacott. It comprises twelve couples of hounds, which hunt the rivers Camel, Thistle, Deer, Bude, Lyd, Claw, Carey, Wolf, Kensey, Waldron, etc., together with tributaries, and good sport is got on the Tamer, Camel, Attery and Okement.

HAWKSTONE

These hounds meet three days a week, the pack having been established many years. The rivers hunted are: the Teme, Wye, Elway, Towy, Cothi, Usk, Clwyd, Corve, together with other rivers and their tributaries. The best of sport is often obtained, as many as sixty otters having been killed in a single season. The kennels are situated on Ludlow racecourse, Bromfield, Salop, and the pack consists of twenty-seven couples of hounds, some being English Foxhounds, Welsh Foxhounds, pure Otterhounds, and others half Fox and half Otter-hounds.

Mr T. P. LEWES'S

Mr Lewes's pack of hounds comprises from eight to ten couples of Welsh hounds and Foxhounds. It is a private pack and hunts the rivers Ayron, Rheidol and Ystwyth, together with various small streams. There are no fixed days of meeting, and otters are not numerous.

PEMBROKESHIRE AND CARMARTHENSHIRE

This is a mixed pack, open to subscription, hunting the rivers in Pembrokeshire and Carmarthenshire,

HOUNDS

MEMBERS OF AN OTTER-HUNT COMPARING NOTES

To face page 158

in which otters are tolerably numerous. The kennels are at Wanngon, Whitland, Pembroke, and contain twelve and a half couples of hounds, the pack being originally formed by officers of the King's Shropshire Light Infantry.

OTTER HOUND.

THE OTTERHOUND

The Otterhound is a shaggy-haired, powerfully built dog, grey grizzle in colour, with deep-set eyes. In early times it was known at the Southern Hound.

They are at their best when hunting, a shaggy mass of pitiless keenness, from which the unfortunate prey finds it most difficult to escape. (*See* ' A Mixed Breed ' p. 83).

They stand 25 inches at the shoulder and weigh 90 lb. Coats hard, long, wiry. An old breed which has been left alone.

There are few pure Otterhound packs ; most packs are composed of Foxhounds, with perhaps a sprinkling of Otterhounds to add to the fascination.

*' He has the peculiar habit,' writes Stonhenge, ' of running over the backs of sheep.' But many sheep dogs do this.—E.C.A.

OTTERHOUND : *Craftsman*, the property of Sir Maurice Bromley-Wilson of Nabwood, Windermere.

THE OTTER HOUND

Origin and History.—Extraordinarily little is known about the history of the otter hound. Some try to link him up with the " otter dogges " used by Edward II, but the general opinion seems to be that the breed is an amalgam of several others in which the Southern hound is predominant. Writing in 1859 Stonehenge, then a leading authority, remarked that : " between a large Welsh harrier and an otter hound no one but an expert could detect any difference, which, after all, will be found only to exist in the coat and feet, and then in a very slight degree. From their constant exposure to the water it is necessary that they should have some further protection than the mere long, open coat of the Welsh Harrier, and no doubt, from selecting those hounds which stood the water best, it has come to pass that the otter hound possesses a thick, piley undercoat, which is, moreover, of a very oily nature." From this quotation we may infer that Stonehenge considered the Welsh Harrier was the channel through which Southern hound blood reached the otter hound.

Standard Description.—However he may have come, we have a handsome, rough-coated hound resembling in many respects the bloodhound, standing 25 or 26 inches at the shoulder. His ears are long as well as his head. The flews are deep and the eyes sometimes show the haw as those of the bloodhound do. The colour may be a grizzle, fawn, blue-and-white or black-and-tan.

It is much to be regretted that few genuine otter hounds survive, most of the packs consisting wholly or mainly of foxhounds. I have not seen one on the show bench for years.

THE OTTERHOUND

THE Otterhound is another of the canine species that has had care bestowed upon it in order to improve its appearance and utility. He is believed to be a descendant of the old southern hound, yet definite proof cannot be given. He is a beautiful animal, with legs and feet that are perfect, and a head as typical as that of a bloodhound.

Bred to hunt otters, which are perhaps the most cunning of all animals, we find these hounds are ideal for the purpose, being steady and methodical. You will see them searching for a trail on rock or boulder, and even if the scent may be one or two days old, they will throw tongue once or twice, and without appearing to hurry will follow the trail, even if it be three or four miles distant. Even if the otter is in a drain 100 yards away from the river, at a depth of 4 feet, they will carry on their work.

Otter-hunting with these hounds is a sport that has been modified, and although the otter finds hard work for men and dogs once he has been unharboured, the hounds will follow him from pool to pool and holt to holt. The spear, however, has now been discontinued, likewise the practice of tailing the otter, thus making it a better and cleaner sport.

OTTERHOUND

The head of an Otterhound should embody the qualities of both the bloodhound and foxhound, yet more hard and rugged than either, with a narrow forehead ascending to a moderate peak. The ears should be long and sweeping, but not feathered down to the tips; they should be set low and lie flat to the cheeks. There should be large dark eyes, set deep, and full of expression, showing a considerable amount of the haw. The nose should be large and well developed, with nostrils expanding; muzzle well protected with wiry hair; strong muscular necks; rather long, deep and capacious chest, but not too wide; strong back, wide and arched, with a stern carried gay, like that of a Welsh harrier. The coat should be wiry, hard, long and close at the roots, impervious to water. The height at shoulder should be 22 to 24 inches.